AF543594

STOIC SECRETS

Unleash the Hidden Power in You!

Published 2025

FiNGERPRINT!

Prakash Books

Fingerprint Publishing
@FingerprintP
@fingerprintpublishingbooks
www.fingerprintpublishing.com

ISBN: 978 93 7089 221 7

Contents

Exploring Stoicism

The Timeless Wisdom We All Need Today

- Stoicism is an ancient Greek philosophy that was founded in Athens by Zeno of Citium in the early third century BCE.

- It teaches development of self-control and fortitude as means of overcoming destructive emotions.

- The philosophy asserts that virtue (such as wisdom) is happiness and that judgment should be based on behavior, rather than words.

- Stoicism emphasizes that we can only control our responses, not external events.

Famous Faces on the Stoic Path

The following personalities inspire and guide individuals in the pursuit of a virtuous and tranquil life continually.

Their quotes encapsulate the essence of Stoic philosophy, emphasizing self-control, rationality and alignment with nature.

"Do you know what's better than building things up in your imagination? Building things up in real life."

RYAN HOLIDAY

Modern author and entrepreneur known for his books on Stoicism, such as *The Obstacle Is the Way* and *Ego Is the Enemy*.

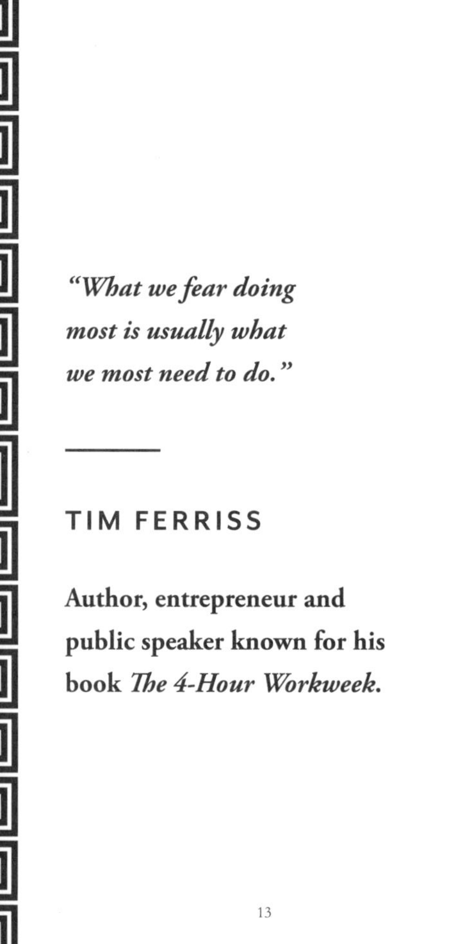

"What we fear doing most is usually what we most need to do."

TIM FERRISS

Author, entrepreneur and public speaker known for his book *The 4-Hour Workweek*.

"Better to endure pain in an honorable manner than to seek joy in a shameful one."

MASSIMO PIGLIUCCI

Professor of Philosophy and author known for his writings on Stoicism, including *How to Be a Stoic*.

"My own practice of Stoicism is very close to that of the ancient Roman Stoics. Although the world has changed since then, human nature is largely unchanged, and Stoicism is all about how to deal with our nature."

WILLIAM B. IRVINE

Professor of Philosophy and author of *A Guide to the Good Life: The Ancient Art of Stoic Joy*.

"Even the Stoic wise man, therefore, may tremble in the face of danger. What matters is what he does next. He exhibits courage and self-control precisely by accepting these feelings, rising above them and asserting his capacity for reason."

DONALD J. ROBERTSON

Cognitive-behavioral psychotherapist and author known for his work on Stoicism, including *How to Think Like a Roman Emperor*.

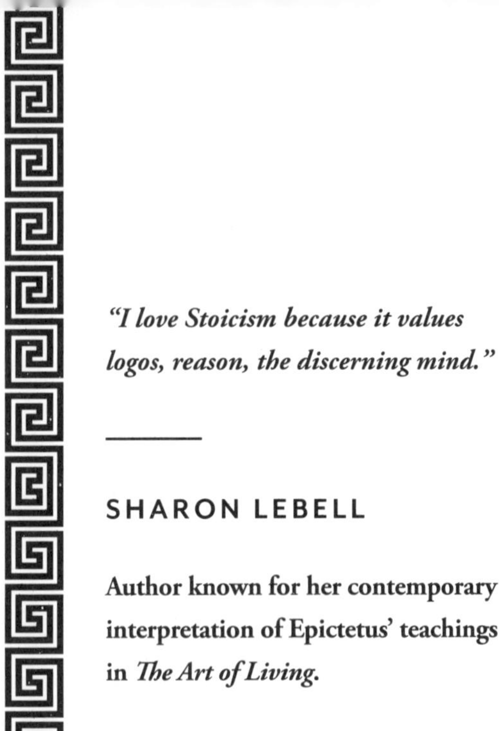

"I love Stoicism because it values logos, reason, the discerning mind."

SHARON LEBELL

Author known for her contemporary interpretation of Epictetus' teachings in *The Art of Living.*

"I'm not a person who defends myself very often. I kind of let my actions speak for me."

TOM BRADY

Professional football player, influenced by Stoic principles. A quarterback known for his disciplined approach to training and life.

"Desire is a contract that you make with yourself to be unhappy until you get what you want."

NAVAL RAVIKANT

Entrepreneur, philosopher, investor and cofounder of the website AngelList that helps startups grow their businesses, also known for his thoughts on Stoicism.

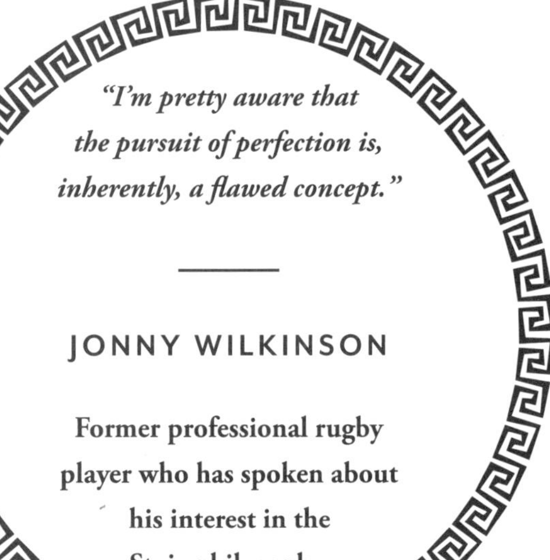

"I'm pretty aware that the pursuit of perfection is, inherently, a flawed concept."

JONNY WILKINSON

Former professional rugby player who has spoken about his interest in the Stoic philosophy.

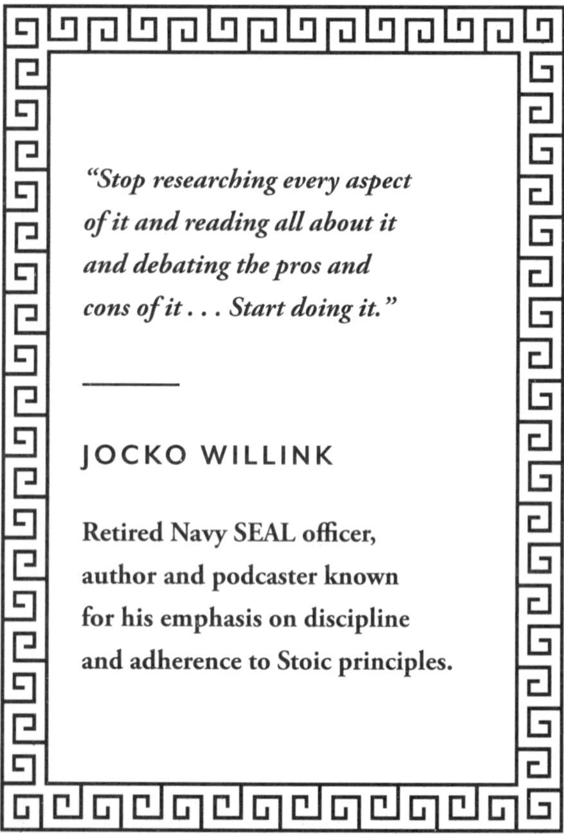

"Stop researching every aspect of it and reading all about it and debating the pros and cons of it . . . Start doing it."

JOCKO WILLINK

Retired Navy SEAL officer, author and podcaster known for his emphasis on discipline and adherence to Stoic principles.

The Stoic Mindset

The Ancient Art of Staying Cool

- Stoicism is like having a mental superhero power: you stay cool under pressure, tackle problems with a calm mind and accept whatever life throws at you with a determined grin. It's about being tough, wise and chill—all at once!

- Stoicism is an ancient philosophy that teaches you how to find inner peace and strength by focusing on what you can control and accepting what you can't.

- It's about developing resilience, staying calm in tough situations and making rational decisions, rather than being driven by emotions.

- Stoics believe in living harmoniously with nature and using reason to navigate life's challenges without being overwhelmed by them.

- It's like having a mental toolkit for handling life's ups and downs with grace and wisdom.

Famous Faces on the Stoic Path

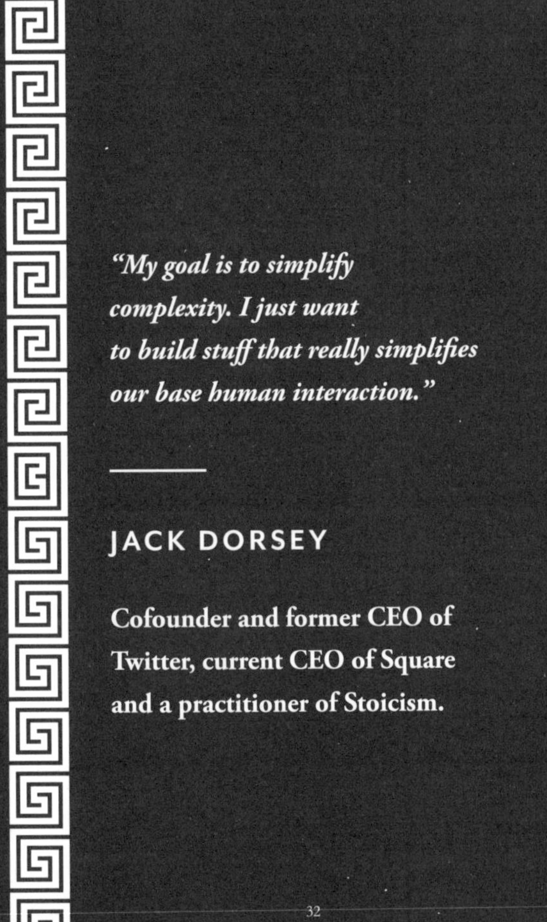

"My goal is to simplify complexity. I just want to build stuff that really simplifies our base human interaction."

JACK DORSEY

Cofounder and former CEO of Twitter, current CEO of Square and a practitioner of Stoicism.

"We need to accept that we won't always make the right decisions, that we'll screw up royally sometimes—understanding that failure is not the opposite of success, it's part of success."

ARIANNA HUFFINGTON

Founder of The Huffington Post and Thrive Global who has spoken about the influence of Stoic philosophy in her life.

"Stay hungry, remain humble and get better today."

PETE CARROLL

Former coach and current advisor of the Seattle Seahawks, known for his use of Stoic principles in coaching and in his life.

"We pursue what we think is good, try to avoid what we think is bad; we feel happy when we get what we think is good, and frustrated when we can't."

JOHN SELLARS

Lecturer in Philosophy and author known for his writings on Stoicism, including *The Art of Living: The Stoics on the Nature and Function of Philosophy.*

"You don't need anyone's approval and in fact, you probably won't get it, so don't even try."

KEVIN ROSE

A practitioner of Stoicism, entrepreneur, venture capitalist and cofounder of the website Digg.

"We are, each of us, a product of the stories we tell ourselves."

DERREN BROWN

Illusionist and author who has written about his use of Stoic principles in his work and life.

"Never forget: This very moment, we can change our lives. There never was a moment, and never will be, when we are without the power to alter our destiny."

STEVEN PRESSFIELD

Author known for his books on writing and creativity, influenced by the Stoic philosophy.

"We are always in a perpetual state of being created and creating ourselves."

DR. DAN SIEGEL

Psychiatrist and author known for his work on mindfulness and its connections to the Stoic philosophy.

*"Wealth consists not
in having great possessions,
but in having few wants."*

EPICTETUS

Ancient Stoic philosopher known for his teachings on Stoic ethics and personal freedom.

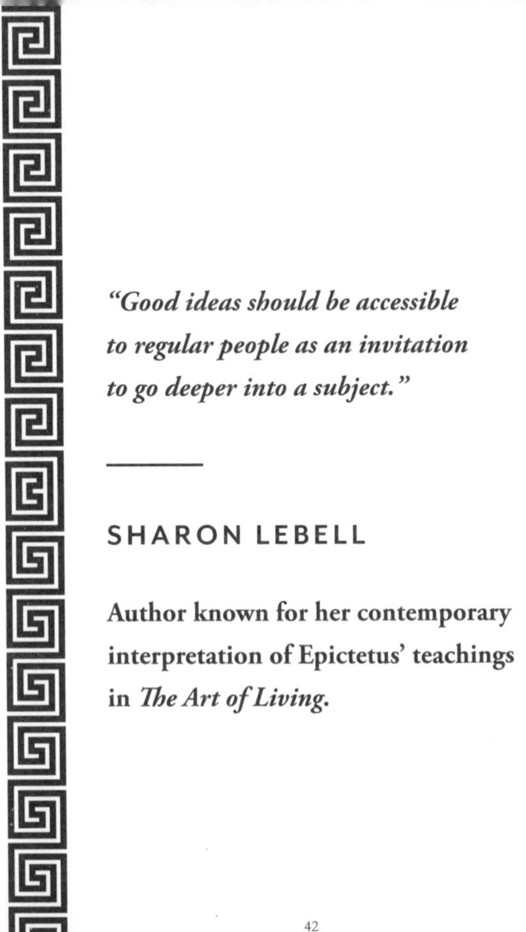

"Good ideas should be accessible to regular people as an invitation to go deeper into a subject."

SHARON LEBELL

Author known for her contemporary interpretation of Epictetus' teachings in *The Art of Living*.

Stoicism 101

What's It All About?

- Stoicism teaches us that we should focus on what is within our control (our thoughts, actions and attitudes), accept what we cannot control (external events) and cultivate virtues like wisdom, courage, justice and moderation.

- The philosophy profoundly influenced the Western thought process and continues to be studied for its practical wisdom and ethical teachings.

- Stoicism asserts that the only true good in life is virtue, which encompasses wisdom, courage, justice and temperance.

- By encouraging you to focus on what is within your control and accept what is not, this principle helps reduce unnecessary stress and anxiety.

- Stoics believe that human beings are rational creatures, and that living in accordance with reason leads to a harmonious and fulfilling life.

- Stoicism helps you understand and align yourself with the natural order of the world that is accepting the laws of nature and the universe.

- Be fully present in the moment and mindful of your thoughts and actions.

- Stoicism helps in making thoughtful and deliberate choices by helping you develop the ability to withstand and recover from adversity. It teaches that our reactions to events, rather than the events themselves, determine our experiences.

- The principle lets you concentrate on your efforts and intentions rather than the outcomes, as the results are often beyond your control.

- Stoicism encourages you to try and achieve tranquility and inner peace by managing desires and maintaining a balanced perspective on life's challenges.

- When you subscribe to Stoicism you regularly reflect on your actions, thoughts and motivations to ensure they align with your values and virtues.

- Stoics treat others with kindness, fairness and understanding, recognizing the presence of imperfections in all human beings.

By adhering to these principles, Stoicism offers a framework for living a virtuous, balanced and resilient life, providing timeless wisdom for navigating the complexities of the human experience.

Famous Faces on the Stoic Path

"It's something I've always found intuitive: You need to tune out the rest of the world to get something truly good accomplished. But it's much easier said than done. Cutting through the noise is a key focus of Stoic thinking."

MEREDITH KUNZ

Writer and author known for her blog The Stoic Mom who applies Stoic principles to parenting.

“We assume that we own things—family, wealth, position—whereas we have only borrowed them from Fortune.”

JAMES ROMM

Professor of the Classics at Bard College and author known for his writings on Stoicism and ancient philosophy.

"The discipline of action is the second phase in Epictetus' sequential, three-phase training program. So, if you're skipping this, you're cutting Stoic practice short."

GREGORY LOPEZ

Coauthor of *A Handbook for New Stoics* and founder of the New York City Stoics.

"Our life is what our thoughts make it."

MARCUS AURELIUS

Roman emperor and philosopher best known for his work *Meditations*, which reflects his Stoic philosophy and insights on leadership and personal virtue.

"Stoicism occupies the middle ground between 'destiny is completely determined by a causal chain' and 'destiny is formed at random.'"

KAI WHITING

Researcher and author known for his work on Stoicism and sustainability.

"A confused mind
is one that is open to the
possibility of change."

ERIC WEINER

Author known for his book *The Socrates Express*, which explores how ancient philosophies, including Stoicism, can be applied to modern life.

"We are at home in the world, they insisted, when we are connected to each other in cooperative efforts. We build resilience and goodness through our deepest relationships."

NANCY SHERMAN

Professor of philosophy and author of *Stoic Warriors*, which examines Stoicism in the military.

"There is a time and place for maximum effort—yes, that's a Deadpool reference—and there's a time and place for stillness and calm."

LAWRENCE BECKER

Philosopher and author of *A New Stoicism*, which modernizes the Stoic thought.

"If we can't control the contents of our consciousness and tame those gremlins of fear and anxiety and self-doubt, none of the rest of this stuff matters. Period."

BRIAN JOHNSON

Philosopher and CEO of Heroic Public Benefit Corporation, known for his teachings on ancient wisdom and modern science.

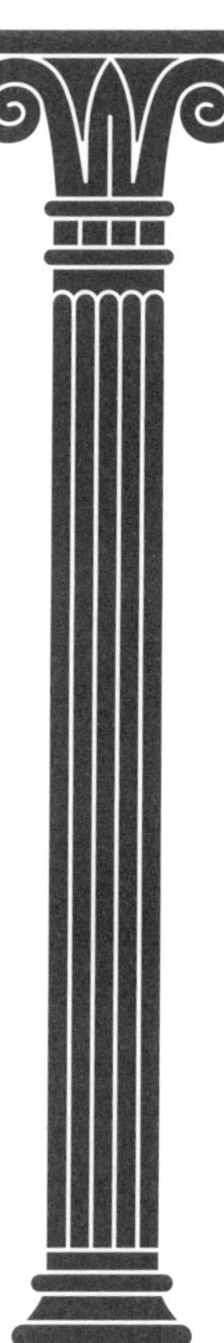

"Socrates had no system to teach. Throughout, his philosophy was a spiritual exercise, an invitation to a new way of life, active reflection and living consciousness."

PIERRE HADOT

Philosopher and historian known for his work on ancient philosophical practices, including Stoicism.

Wisdom from the Stoics

Tips You'll Want to Hear

Are you dealing with drama while navigating the modern maze of life?

Stoicism has your back with its blend of cool, ancient and timeless wisdom! It teaches you to bounce back stronger from setbacks and adversity, turning life's lemons into philosophical lemonade.

- Stoics are masters of keeping calm under pressure. They teach you how to handle life's curveballs without losing your cool; it's like having a mental fortress against stress. Practice *negative visualization*. Imagine potential challenges or setbacks in advance, so when they happen, you're not caught off guard. This reduces anxiety and helps you stay calm.

- Stoics are all about being their best self. They'll help you level up your moral game with virtues like wisdom, courage, justice and self-control. Break down each day into smaller actions. Ask yourself, "Is this action aligned with courage, wisdom, justice or self-control?" Constant self-checking keeps you aligned with your values.

- They've cracked the code to happiness. By teaching you to focus on what you can control—your thoughts and actions—Stoics show you how to find contentment regardless of external chaos. Make a list of things that worry or stress you out. Divide them into two categories: things within your control (like your actions) and things beyond your control (other people's opinions, the weather). Focus only on what you can influence.

- Stoics guide you in developing resilience and prepare you to walk through adversity with strength and grace. Reframe setbacks as opportunities for growth. Instead of seeing failure as the end, ask yourself, "What can I learn from this?"

- Stoics teach you to stay composed under pressure so that you can handle life's challenges without losing your cool. Practice deep, mindful breathing. When faced with a high-pressure situation, take a few deep breaths to ground yourself before responding.

- Find inner tranquility by accepting what you cannot change and focusing on your responses. Practice letting go. When something is out of your hands, remind yourself, "This is beyond my control, and my energy is better spent elsewhere."

- Stoics teach you to make wise, thoughtful decisions grounded in rationality and reason. Use the *Stoic pause*. Before making any decision, pause to consider the long-term consequences and whether it aligns with your principles.

- They help you master your impulses and emotions, leading to a more disciplined and fulfilling life. Track your emotional triggers. Identify moments when you're likely to lose control and have strategies in place (like stepping away or taking a deep breath) to manage those emotions.

- Stoics guide you as you learn to enhance focus and mindfulness by prioritizing the present moment. Practice *mindful presence.*

Throughout the day, bring your attention back to the present moment. Focus fully on whatever task you're doing, whether it's eating, walking or working.

- You learn to build better relationships from them through understanding, empathy and fairness. Practice empathy by putting yourself in the other person's shoes before reacting. Ask, "How would I feel if I were in their situation?"

- Engage in regular self-reflection and growth, constantly aligning your actions with your values. At the end of each day, practice *evening reflection*. Ask yourself, "What did I do well today? Where could I improve?" This keeps you aligned with your values and on the path of self-growth.

Stoic teachings have stood the test of time. From ancient Athens to modern-day hustle, Stoic insights are like a timeless life manual, offering practical advice for a fulfilling existence.

Famous Faces on the Stoic Path

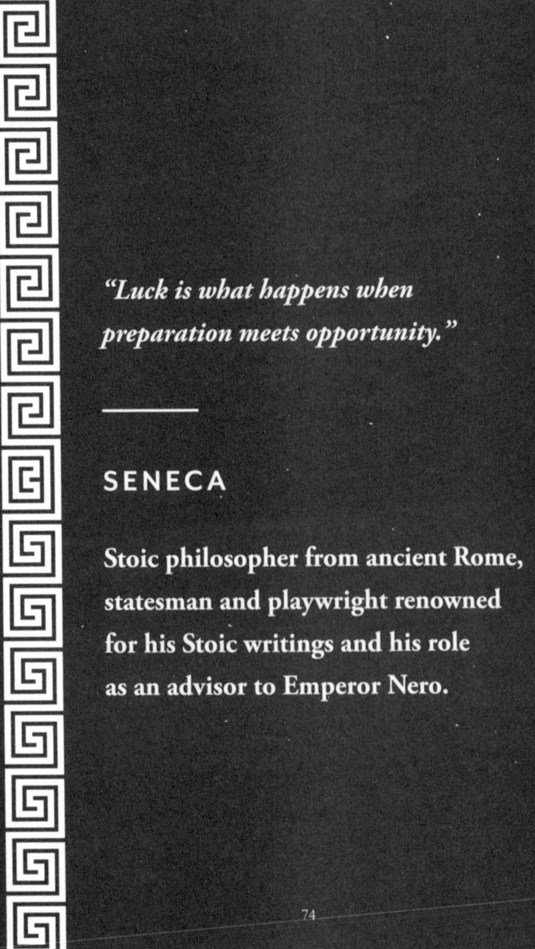

"Luck is what happens when preparation meets opportunity."

SENECA

Stoic philosopher from ancient Rome, statesman and playwright renowned for his Stoic writings and his role as an advisor to Emperor Nero.

"Always remember that your calmness under fire is your best defense in any argument or discussion."

ROBERT GREENE

Author of *The 48 Laws of Power* and *The Daily Laws*, exploring Stoic principles for over thirty years.

"The person who is truly best suited to us is not the person who shares our tastes, but the person who can negotiate differences in taste intelligently and wisely."

ALAIN DE BOTTON

Philosopher, author and founder of the website The School of Life, which integrates Stoic principles in its published materials.

"While any adversity could strike us, it's how we respond that is a measure of our true character."

DAVID FIDELER

Philosopher and author of *Breakfast with Seneca,* studied ancient religions and philosophies with the history of science.

"You will discover not only that you can weather challenges, but you often find them enjoyable."

MATT VAN NATTA

Host of the podcast *Good Fortune* and author of *The Beginner's Guide to Stoicism.*

"It's natural to have doubts, fears, and uncertainties, but it's how we respond to them that matters. The first step to responding to our negative thoughts is recognizing them and understanding why we want to change."

ERIC ZIMMER

Behavior coach and podcast host of *The One You Feed*, explores human behavior through Stoic lenses.

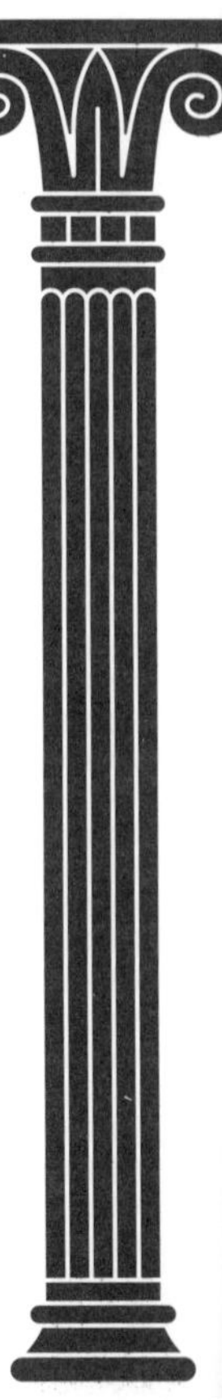

"Man conquers the world by conquering himself."

ZENO OF CITIUM

Ancient philosopher and the founder of Stoic philosophy.

"When someone is properly grounded in life, they shouldn't have to look outside themselves for approval."

EPICTETUS

Ancient Stoic philosopher known for his teachings on Stoic ethics and personal freedom.

"So, if we want to live a good life, the most important thing we need to do is to attend to ourselves, to how we think about things (back to our judgements again) and what we think has most value."

JOHN SELLARS

Lecturer in Philosophy and author known for his writings on Stoicism, including *The Art of Living: The Stoics on the Nature and Function of Philosophy.*

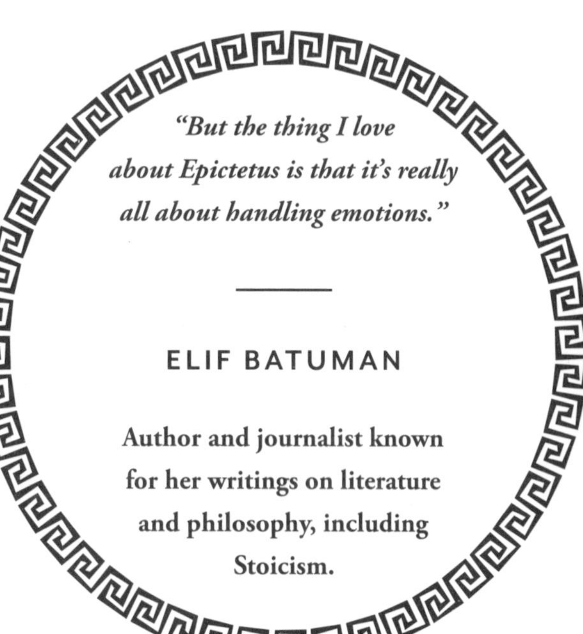

"But the thing I love about Epictetus is that it's really all about handling emotions."

ELIF BATUMAN

Author and journalist known for her writings on literature and philosophy, including Stoicism.

Stoicism in a Nutshell

The Core Beliefs

- Stoics emphasize distinguishing between what is within our control and what is not. Acceptance of things outside our control is crucial.

- Stoicism teaches that human beings are rational, and that our emotions often stem from our own false judgments.

- Stoicism encourages focusing on the present moment rather than being overwhelmed by the past or future.

- Stoicism advises regular contemplation of death and the transience of life to foster appreciation and mindfulness.

- Stoics believe in changing one's perception of adverse events and to view them as opportunities for growth and learning.

- Stoics advocate living harmoniously with others and building comradeship among all of humanity.

- Stoics encourage regular reflection upon one's thoughts and actions to ensure they align with Stoic virtues.

- One of the principle characteristic of Stoicism is understanding that external goods (wealth, fame, etc.) are superficial and do not contribute to true happiness.

- Maintaining a balanced emotional state by not allowing external events to disturb one's inner peace is a key element of being a Stoic.

- Stoics believe in taking deliberate and purposeful actions that are aligned with virtue and reason.

- Stoics develop the strength to endure hardships and maintain tranquility in the face of adversity.

- Practicing gratitude for what one has and focusing on the positives rather than what is lacking is also an important aspect of being a Stoic.

- Stoics apply the Stoic principles in their lives extensively to lead a life of integrity, fairness and moral clarity.

Famous Faces on the Stoic Path

"If people have a passion for anything they tend to get quite good at it."

BRIAN JOHNSON

Philosopher and CEO of Heroic Public Benefit Corporation, known for his teachings on ancient wisdom and modern science.

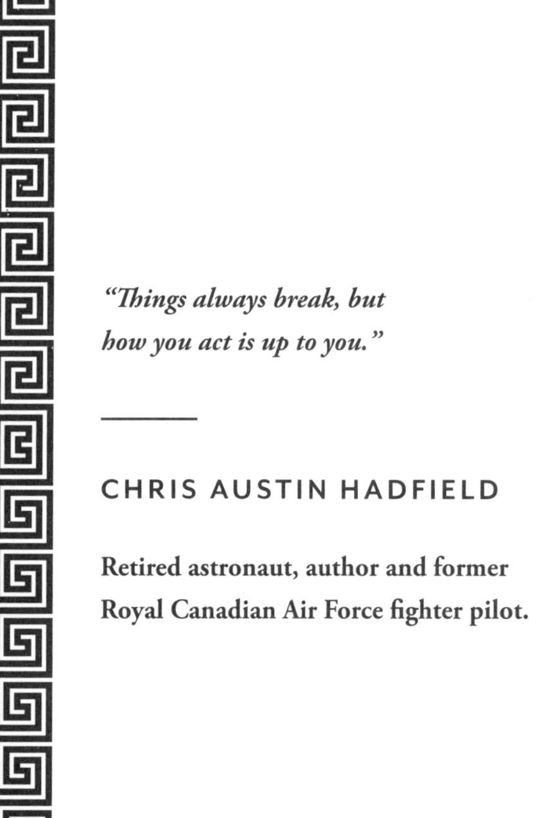

"Things always break, but how you act is up to you."

CHRIS AUSTIN HADFIELD

Retired astronaut, author and former Royal Canadian Air Force fighter pilot.

"An authentic personality characterizes people by their actions and is never fooled by their words no matter how sugary those are."

LACHLAN BROWN

Founder of the website Hack Spirit where he integrates Stoic principles with his teachings on mindfulness and self-improvement.

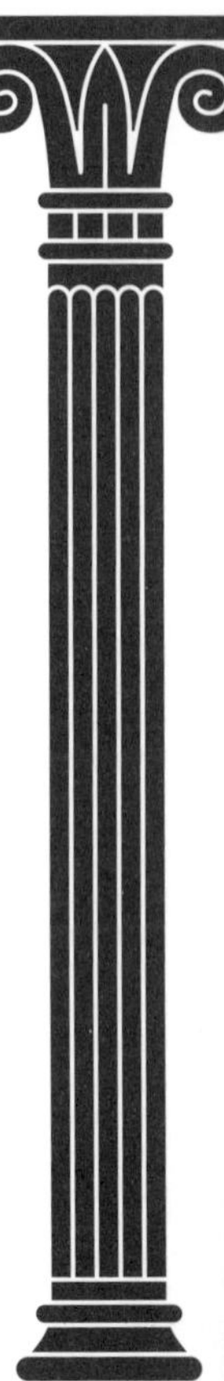

"Your mind is for having ideas, not holding them."

DAVID ALLEN

Productivity consultant and author of *Getting Things Done* where he relates Stoic principles with productivity.

"In the end, people are persuaded not by what we say, but by what they understand."

JOHN MAXWELL

Leadership expert and author incorporating Stoic principles into his teachings on leadership.

"The angry person is acutely sensitive to all they are owed by the world, and blind to all they have received."

JULES EVANS

Author and philosopher known for his work on Stoicism and well-being.

"What I've found in my research is that realism and self-honesty are the antidote to ego, hubris and delusion."

RYAN HOLIDAY

Modern author and entrepreneur known for his books on Stoicism, such as *The Obstacle Is the Way* and *Ego Is the Enemy*.

*"I can't speak for others,
but I find the fundamental
idea that a life worth living
is one during which one strives
every day to become a better
person to be compelling."*

MASSIMO PIGLIUCCI

Professor of Philosophy and author known for his writings on Stoicism, including *How to Be a Stoic*.

"You have power over your mind—not outside events. Realize this, and you will find strength."

MARCUS AURELIUS

Roman emperor and philosopher best known for his work *Meditations*, which reflects his Stoic philosophy and insights on leadership and personal virtue.

"The first principle of practical Stoicism is this: we don't react to events; we react to our judgments about them, and the judgments are up to us."

WARD FARNSWORTH

Former dean of the University of Texas School of Law and author of *The Practicing Stoic*.

"A true artist, in my mind, is willing to fail sometimes, because if you're not brave enough to say yes and follow your gut, it's never going to be good."

ALEXANDER SKARSGÅRD

Actor known for playing several Stoic characters, has discussed finding inspiration in Stoic philosophy, particularly in maintaining perspective and balance amid the pressures of fame.

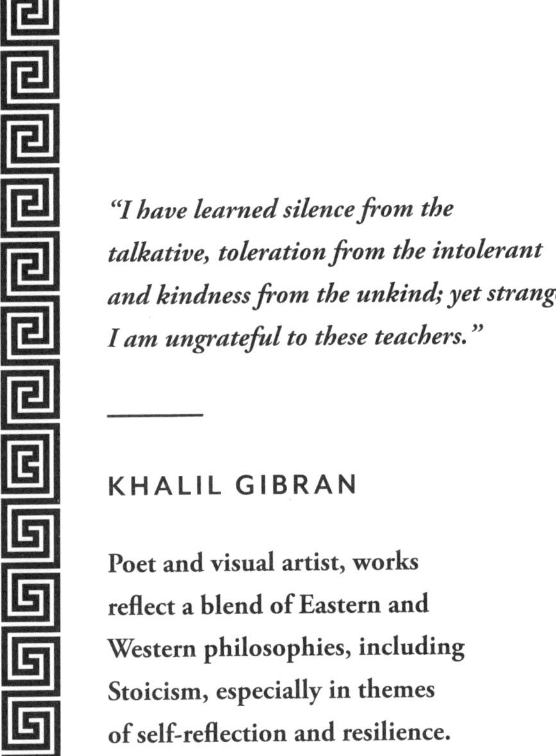

"I have learned silence from the talkative, toleration from the intolerant and kindness from the unkind; yet strange, I am ungrateful to these teachers."

KHALIL GIBRAN

Poet and visual artist, works reflect a blend of Eastern and Western philosophies, including Stoicism, especially in themes of self-reflection and resilience.

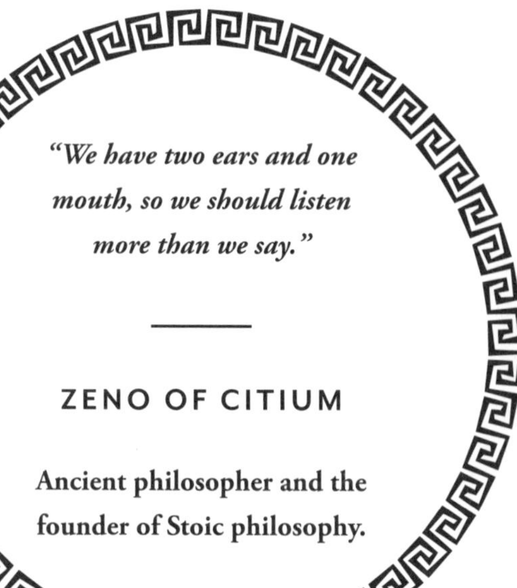

"We have two ears and one mouth, so we should listen more than we say."

ZENO OF CITIUM

Ancient philosopher and the founder of Stoic philosophy.

"God grant me the serenity to accept the things I cannot change, courage to change the things I can, and wisdom to know the difference."

REINHOLD NIEBUHR

Political commentator, author and professor.

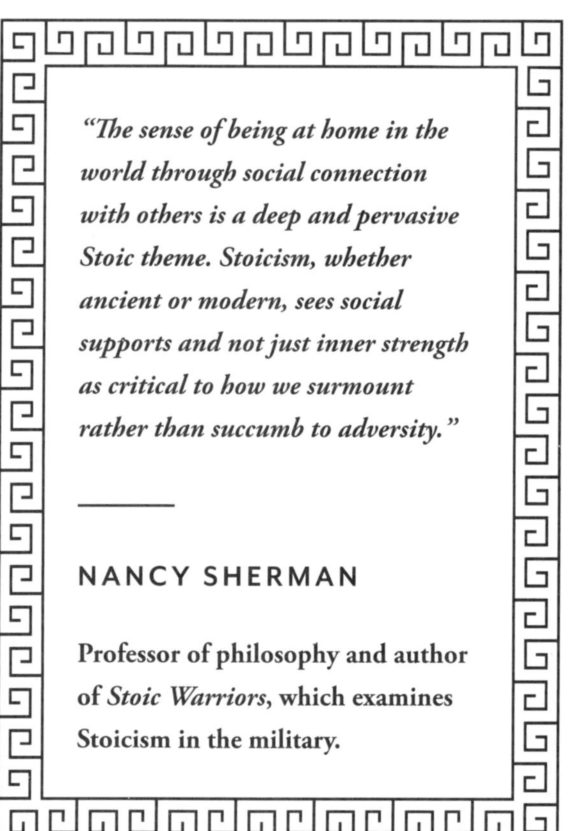

"The sense of being at home in the world through social connection with others is a deep and pervasive Stoic theme. Stoicism, whether ancient or modern, sees social supports and not just inner strength as critical to how we surmount rather than succumb to adversity."

NANCY SHERMAN

Professor of philosophy and author of *Stoic Warriors*, which examines Stoicism in the military.

"For Stoicism, it's a smooth-flowing life in accordance with nature which is equivalent with eudaimonia."

GREGORY LOPEZ

Coauthor of *A Handbook for New Stoics* and founder of the New York City Stoics.

"Guilt is the uncomfortable certainty that we are not what we could have been."

MICHAEL SUGRUE

Historian and lecturer, was known for his teachings on Stoicism and ancient philosophy.

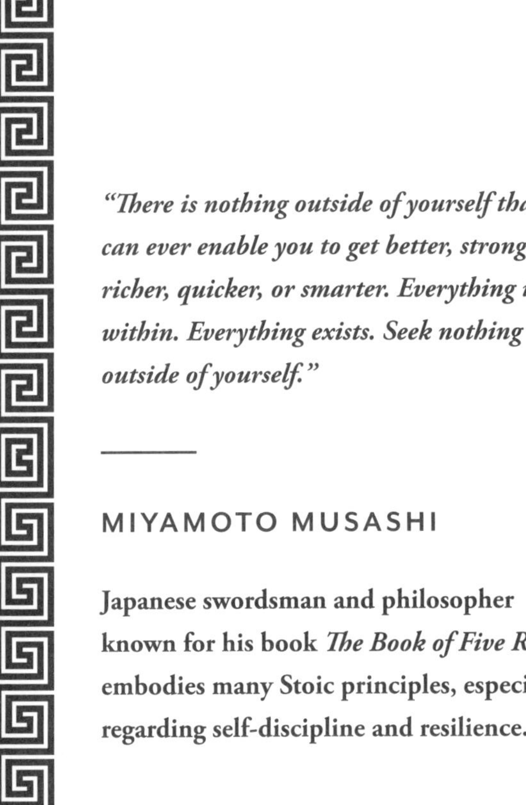

"There is nothing outside of yourself that can ever enable you to get better, stronger, richer, quicker, or smarter. Everything is within. Everything exists. Seek nothing outside of yourself."

MIYAMOTO MUSASHI

Japanese swordsman and philosopher known for his book *The Book of Five Rings* embodies many Stoic principles, especially regarding self-discipline and resilience.

"The only thing each of us lives and loses is the present."

PIERRE HADOT

Philosopher and historian known for his work on ancient philosophical practices, including Stoicism.

"As someone who is very much into Zen Buddhism, Stoicism is probably the closest thing to it in the Western sense. What's so nice about it is that it's not only a hardcore philosophy but it's also quite poetic. It makes you contemplate the weirdness of life and the sublimity of things."

ROBERT GREENE

Author of *The 48 Laws of Power* and *The Daily Laws*, exploring Stoic principles for over thirty years.

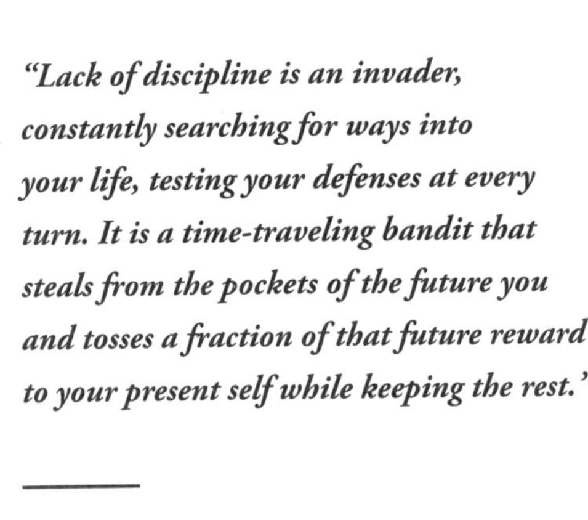

"Lack of discipline is an invader, constantly searching for ways into your life, testing your defenses at every turn. It is a time-traveling bandit that steals from the pockets of the future you and tosses a fraction of that future reward to your present self while keeping the rest."

CHRIS FISHER

Host of the podcast *Stoicism on Fire*, which explores Stoic philosophy in everyday life.

"All men make mistakes, but a good man yields when he knows his course is wrong and repairs the evil. The only crime is pride."

SOPHOCLES

Ancient Greek playwright, famous for his tragedies like *Oedipus Rex* and *Antigone*, which explored complex themes of fate, morality and human suffering.

"More is lost by indecision than wrong decision."

MARCUS TULLIUS CICERO

Roman statesman, orator and philosopher known for his speeches, writings on rhetoric and philosophy and his efforts to uphold the Roman Republic during its decline.

"If you accomplish something good with hard work, the labor passes quickly, but the good endures; if you do something shameful in pursuit of pleasure, the pleasure passes quickly, but the shame endures."

GAIUS MUSONIUS RUFUS

Roman Stoic philosopher and teacher known for his practical teachings on ethics, advocating for simplicity, self-discipline and the equality of women in philosophy.

"It takes a wise man
to discover a wise man."

DIOGENES

Ancient Greek philosopher and one of the most famous Cynics, often living in a barrel and challenging the norms of his time.

"While we are postponing, life speeds by."

SENECA

Stoic philosopher from ancient Rome, statesman and playwright renowned for his Stoic writings and his role as an advisor to Emperor Nero.

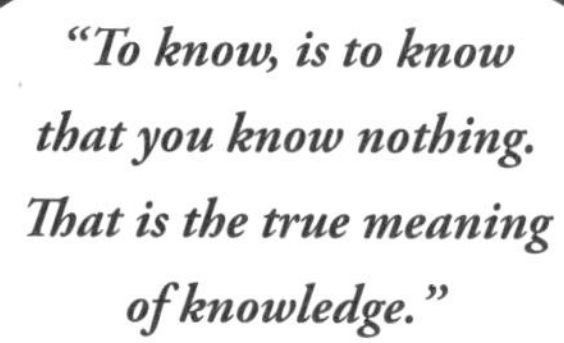

"To know, is to know that you know nothing. That is the true meaning of knowledge."

SOCRATES

Ancient Greek philosopher known as the founder of Western philosophy.

"If you care enough for a result, you will most certainly attain it."

WILLIAM JAMES

An influential American philosopher and psychologist known for his contributions to the philosophy of pragmatism and pioneering work in the psychology of consciousness and religious experience.

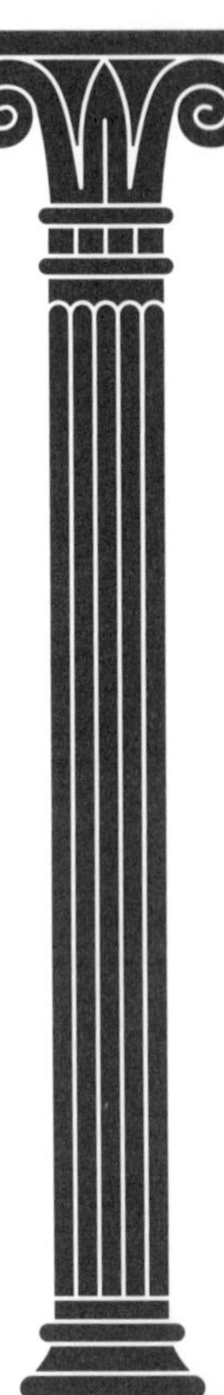

"Life is ten percent what happens to you and ninety percent how you respond to it."

LOU HOLTZ

Legendary American football coach known for his successful tenure at the University of Notre Dame, leading the team to a national championship in 1988.

"You are in danger of living a life so comfortable and soft that you will die without ever realizing your true potential."

DAVID GOGGINS

Retired Navy SEAL, ultramarathon runner and author.

"I don't think there's an interesting boundary between philosophy and science. Science is totally beholden to philosophy. There are philosophical assumptions in science and there's no way to get around that."

SAM HARRIS

Neuroscientist, philosopher, podcast host and author.

*"That's my only goal.
Surround myself with funny people and make sure everyone has a good time and works hard."*

JOE ROGAN

Comedian, UFC commentator and television and podcast host.

*"Prioritize who you are,
who you want to be, and don't
spend time with anything that
antagonizes your character."*

MATTHEW McCONAUGHEY

Actor and author, influenced by Stoic principles.

"Chains of habit are too light to be felt until they are too heavy to be broken."

WARREN BUFFETT

Investor and philanthropist who incorporates Stoic principles in his decision-making.

"You can't connect the dots looking forward; you can only connect them looking backwards. So you have to trust that the dots will somehow connect in your future. You have to trust in something—your gut, destiny, life, karma, whatever. This approach has never let me down, and it has made all the difference in my life."

STEVE JOBS

Cofounder of Apple, known for his practice of Stoic resilience.

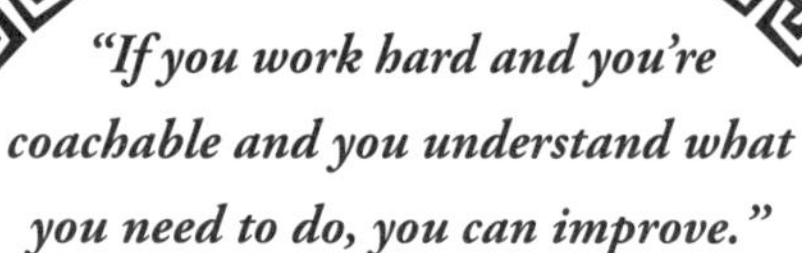

"If you work hard and you're coachable and you understand what you need to do, you can improve."

BILL BELICHICK

Sports analyst and former NFL coach of the New England Patriots, follows Stoic concepts.

"When you view failure as feedback, you get more done. When you view failure as a finality, you get nothing done."

JACK BUTCHER

Entrepreneur and creator of Visualize Value website, focuses on Stoic wisdom.

"Learning to give up on perfection may be just about the most romantic move any of us could make."

ALAIN DE BOTTON

Philosopher, author and founder of the website The School of Life, which integrates Stoic principles in its published materials.

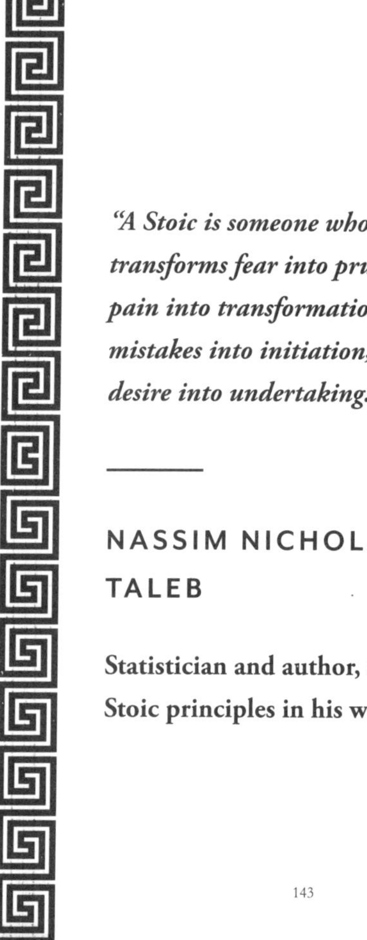

"A Stoic is someone who transforms fear into prudence, pain into transformation, mistakes into initiation, and desire into undertaking."

NASSIM NICHOLAS TALEB

Statistician and author, applies Stoic principles in his works.

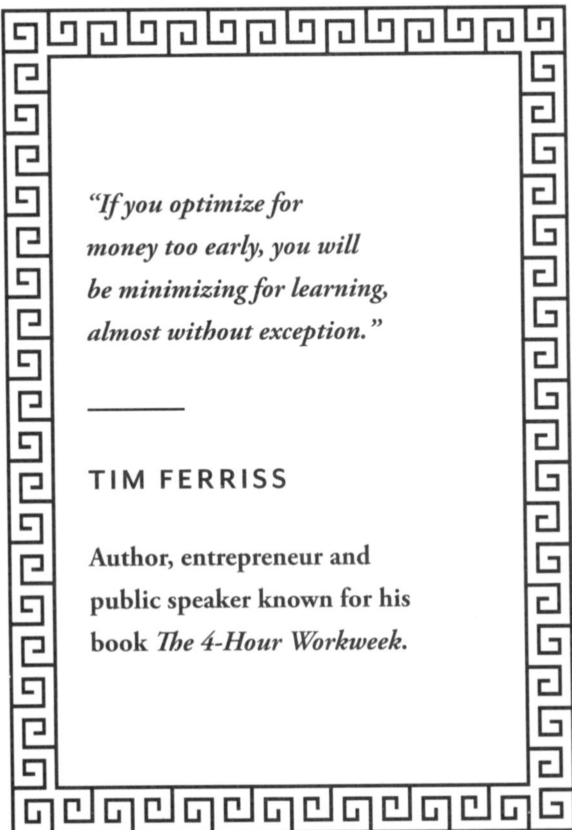

"If you optimize for money too early, you will be minimizing for learning, almost without exception."

TIM FERRISS

Author, entrepreneur and public speaker known for his book *The 4-Hour Workweek*.

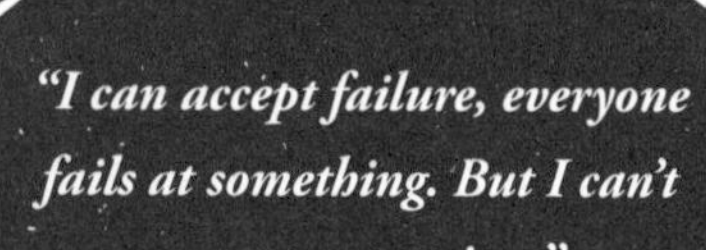

"I can accept failure, everyone fails at something. But I can't accept not trying."

MICHAEL JORDAN

Former basketball player, known for his disciplined mindset.

"To be beautiful means to be yourself. You don't need to be accepted by others. You need to accept yourself."

THICH NHAT HANH

Vietnamese Zen master emphasized mindfulness and presence, which align with Stoic ideas about focusing on the present and controlling one's reactions.

"Innate within all of us lies the ability to shift into the identity that enables us to unlock a new level of power, perspective, passion, productivity and to be successful in life."

ANTHONY TRUCKS

Former NFL player and motivational speaker.

"Let's start as small as we need to start so you can get consistent."

ERIC ZIMMER

Behavior coach and podcast host of *The One You Feed*, explores human behavior through Stoic lenses.

"Every choice you make
is a step toward or away from
the person you want to become."

SHANE PARRISH

Blogger, podcaster and author of *Clear Thinking* and other books, influenced by Stoic principles.

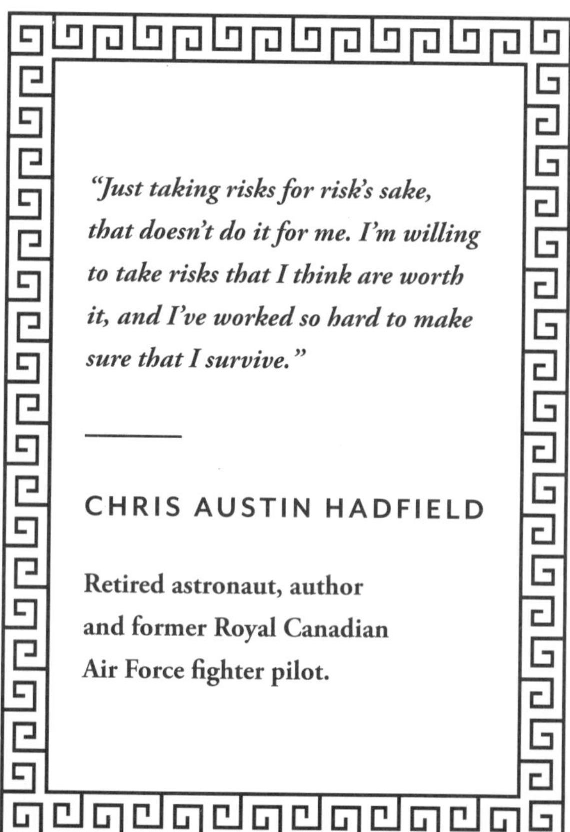

"Just taking risks for risk's sake, that doesn't do it for me. I'm willing to take risks that I think are worth it, and I've worked so hard to make sure that I survive."

CHRIS AUSTIN HADFIELD

Retired astronaut, author and former Royal Canadian Air Force fighter pilot.

"Plant the seeds of greatness in your mind."

JAMES CLEAR

Author of *Atomic Habits*, emphasizing Stoic habits.

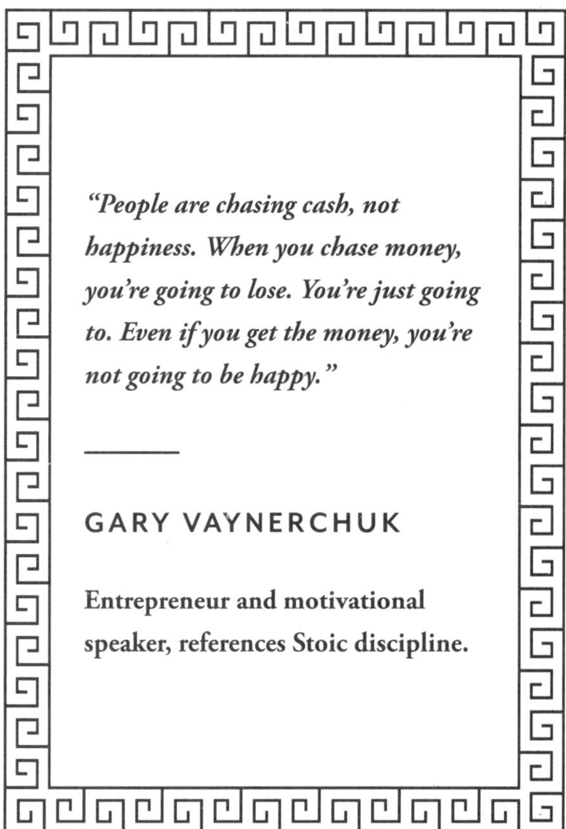

"People are chasing cash, not happiness. When you chase money, you're going to lose. You're just going to. Even if you get the money, you're not going to be happy."

GARY VAYNERCHUK

Entrepreneur and motivational speaker, references Stoic discipline.

"Whatever position you're in now, you can change, no matter how horrific, no matter what you've been through, no matter what you've done, there is a way out from under it."

TOM BILYEU

Entrepreneur and founder of Impact Theory, follows Stoic ideas.

"When the mind is controlled and spirit aligned with purpose, the body is capable of so much more than we realize."

RICH ROLL

Author, ultra-endurance athlete and podcaster.

"We need the compassion and the courage to change the conditions that support our suffering. Those conditions are things like ignorance, bitterness, negligence, clinging and holding on."

SHARON SALZBERG

Meditation teacher and author, embraces Stoic values.

"We don't control our initial reaction, perhaps, but we do control how we respond to it: it's not what happens first that matters but what you do next."

DONALD J. ROBERTSON

Cognitive-behavioral psychotherapist and author known for his work on Stoicism, including *How to Think Like a Roman Emperor*.